TOWN

Published 2005
by

BOOKS

Smokestack Books
PO Box 408, Middlesbrough TS5 6WA
Tel : 01642 813997
e-mail : info@smokestack-books.co.uk
www.smokestack-books.co.uk

Copyright Alan Dent
All rights reserved

Cover image
from a woodcut by Henry Saairnen

Cover design and print by
James Cianciaruso

ISBN 0-9548691-2-5

Smokestack Books
gratefully acknowledges the support of
Middlesbrough Borough Council
and Arts Council North East.

Smokestack Books is a member of
The Independent Northern Publishers
www.northernpublishers.co.uk

TOWN

Alan Dent

For my Daughters

'The English character has failed to develop the real urban side of man, the civic side.'
                                           D. H. Lawrence

'In feverish hordes, the suburbs swarm to the polling booth to vote against a truculent Proletariat.'
                                           C.F.G. Masterman

'Money, like vodka, can play queer tricks with a man.'
                                           Chekhov

'Consciousness, that historical relationship between boat and water.'

                                           Cesar Vallejo

Town

Town

Town inviting town
    town of night light
    togetherness
and nature as humankind has made it
    town our home our undwelling
new primeval forest
    this loom-transformed hilltopped town
smiling to a hilltopped boy dipping
    dizzily to the dirty river and up
up in a weepless sweep to the dirty lovely town.

    And this is where I came to make my life
a corner plot a hedge a lawn a house
  four-bedroomed bigger than the common three
    and married to a man whose brains I thought
    should take him far
                  should let him climb and shine
    we fell below my hopes which I let fall
on my three offspring well-spring of my pride
  the last conceived in beer and oh be damned
an accidental boy in every way
  low oxygen at birth to be the cause
    of his slow mind in all my saving tales
        how else to face
  that this was born of me
    this poor-brained fool set sure to fail my hopes
oh had I known my womb could grow such shame
I would have crushed his tiny new-born head
  or drowned him in a bucket like a runt
    this lump this blob this living lack of worth
  this carthorse born of me a thoroughbred
    no better than the low that live in town
        and slave in factories
    as their birth dictates
    and all my signs of better undermined
by this one fact this ever-present mark
this blot upon election's pristine page
  my son town-brained street-gened
                not one of us.

    And how did I the dirty low town-boy
come to the clear clean suburb
    is nothing safe or sacred

                1955 my dockside dad
                              ten years demobbed
                  got money as the poor always do
        by graft or gift or luck
                        chance chucked my terraced urchin's chin
            plucked me from the mean and treeless streets
        into this paradise of space and grass
                        into this hell of snobs
                and he the son my age of a sniffy town-free mother
            mismatch of the take-it-as-it-comes back-alley kid
        and unloved prove-me-worthy cup-on-the-mantlepiece scion
                        so in that clash of class and attitude
                ignored for friendship's sake
                            (for what mad child will freeze a friend
                    if lonely playfulness like dead eternity
                        is else)
                    a had-its-day past met a breech birth future
                    in groves made monied
                        by the dirty work of the lovely dirty town.

                                    And I was an insurance man her man
            I knew the fine print and the patter
                            how to cover your wife
    (but earth is all I would have covered my own wife with)
                        your life your death
                your ill health and your good health
    your children and your wealth and your children's wealth
            and your children's children's wealth
                        your house its contents
            and the contents of its contents
                    insured against all loss theft and perdition
    insured to hell
            like a prayer to heaven
                        and heaven was a woman half my age
    who had a leisure in her way and voice
                that calmed my blood
            and cooled my poor head's fever
    pain that rose from my tight gripping neck
    when her sharp voice
                    a jagged-toothed whistling saw
            whirred through my nerves
                    her will to argument
    a million vicious volts arrowing through my arteries
    the poor trapped bird of my heart flapping for release
                        one policy I should have taken out

                against a bitter woman
        so sweet the spent-out hours
            working day
        but oh the loving night
                April sun on frozen snow of my iglooed marriage
                  this primrose in the brambles
      this lick of ice in desert's midday parch

      how did she know

        just this she said to me that she just knew
the quiet in me
      my blood's slow fuse at her goad of command
(my hard yet hard enough
            and at her bid
    perfunctory detached
      unminded)
    and found us out one afternoon
              lasered
    from pub to pub
    each café scoured for signs
          together like a simple pair of kids
as if her bed unhusbanded and mine
                  unwifed.

We'll move.

I had to leave
to stand one final happiness with her
        on the dry flat shore
    by the distant quiet sea
            one last peak of heart's-peace
before the grey expanse of lovelessness
    encircled me as far as hope could see
and all I'd ever gaze on
    the dry unflowered landscape
        blown over by the dusty winds
of blank recrimination.

So we came to the big square house on the hill
        big square couple
    couple in the big square house
with our big square minds
        and our four square children
    four sides of our big square world

six sides of the blank cube of our getting-on existence
        and we were getting on
    up here on the pleasant hill
in the big square house with the big square garage
      for our big square car
    and the big square school
          with all the requisites of big square status
(the Latin motto buggery and rugger)
        and so I mowed the big square lawn
and smiled the smile that showed my big square teeth
    and laughed my big square laugh
and when I lost my angled temper
        hit my eldest with my big square hands
      and in the whole round world
the infinitely circular back-upon-itself universe
nothing was so square as our arena
the straight lines in which we talked and thought
    our parallelogrammic love
    the right-angles of our sharp opinions
the clear diagonals of our geometric ambitions.

      If one ambition gnawed me
    it was to see her in her cask
to see the brass screws tighten
        like the squeeze of money
    to see the trite equipment trundle her
        through the comme il faut curtains
to eternity.

```
        As if eternity might serve time's servant
                    (town-boy my wisdom was
                  the stars aren't ours
        and separate here
                 cast up by causes blind as we to them
             unanchored to our origins
we're a breath, a breeze,
                 a rustle in the midnight treetops
            heard an unsung second
gone
            into the black silence of was once)
       a transience to treasure
the quick flow and swing of life
            bred for the bike the brook
the book left for its time tight in the hallway case
        limbed for the lovely moment
```

                    my brainlinks on fire with
being's simple interestingness
                    dead to dead time
    time of the factory's metronome
the schoolroom's regulated hours
    ambition's heart-defeating dullness
        life sacrificed to life to come
    that never comes
    the ever-postponement of the moment's fullness
        for lucre-lure
            statue-status
        corseted petty despotism
success-sick worth-proving warmed-over Calvinism
    vicious creed of prim credulous mindsuburbs
  trimmed as neat as hedges
        electric shears of snobbery
    slicing each stray leaf
                long-handled snip of sniffiness
nipping the tip of each lush sappy shaft of grass.

                    A winter morning
bright
    sharp
        blue
    and each touched blade
            taut with painted frost
the skidding ball and the steaming breath
        and glow-cheeked panting into class
    thirty unsure futures
Parisian ambassador or Dorman Smith dogsbody
        engineer of piston precision
    or lifetime prison prowler
husbanded housewife whose wishes waft with her whites
    or world-wise money-whore whose innocence
sinks as her bonuses soar.

        Two miles out of town
    neighbour-wooded
            fielded for the swooping summer swifts
        my town-boy's happiness was here
winging ball-footed in a couldn't-care-less-who-wins
    sweet sensuousness of white-line bounded
            strict-ruled play
running mud-soled the rhododendroned woods
    walking green befriended miles

idyll of dawdling idleness.

And I the scion of the big square house
heaped with big square ambitions
    wrought in a wrack
   of winner-takes-all
lifted from sureness of self
    speaking to myself in lies
    lying lonely with ambition for my love
       dreamed of absolution absolute
       in money-success's certain worthiness
    as if a life's worth weighs against another
        coin-costed
    note-notched
    in counterfeited counting
    cruel accountancy of the heart's calculus
        ill-seen actuarialism
       misery of misplaced calculation
    trap of the cash-till's stilling autism.

And it was a knife
       that sharp ribsticking pushing me
  that jab of I
     that blank flat nothingness of all
as if the stars were in my head
        as if I were the limit and the range of life
   not little ringed-about and real
     like town-boy
friend of flux and fleet
     his me as light as light
   as gone as breath
     the speaking of his being like a happy phrase
the chance of rhyme
       the lucky skip of rhythm in the brain
   the accident of here his health
the trip of now
     a set of happenings set by who knows what
   and in that flip that play
     that lovely sliver caught where past butts future
was his joy
   his live the day and let it go
     but live it well
       raising my blood to spite
   in my too false foregoing of life's flash
my fixing of my me
        as if time wouldn't ride it like a toy

             as if a me is ever and not now
                      as if not made
             from making of our life together
         sweet solidness of flesh and earth and bark
   loveliness of concrete and of steel
             and town
         built to stay a second in sun's calendar.

             And she
         sweet shock of beauty
                   that out-of-nowhere miracle
                of eyes and nose and mouth symmetrical
         a face to power rockets to the moon
                   out-of-the-world loveliness
             here in the everyday world
                as if a little school in Crookings Lane
         could sculpt a Cleopatra
             and what was life but this
         the sudden firing of a soaring joy
                to last till age
             and what was age but this
         the smiling memory of the sudden joy
         that fired soared and touched the stars
                   and fell back slowly
                driftingly through years of sweet decline
             to earth
                she whose accidental loveliness
         touched every tender nerve in my town mind
                   whose sad blue eyes askance
                catching my blue eyes
                   lowered with shy flicker of a smile
   was snob-raised
                cast in square-boy's mould
       in whose unroving eye she lived
   only in sad worth-pursuit's mad panic
         so didn't live at all
         and everything that might have been a life
   that might have made a little common joy
                      was gathered into this tight knot
             of striving for a final proof of worth
                   that froze all loveliness of life
         and fixed a hard cold eye upon
                         false measures of election
             in this false place upon its hill
             as if its nose rose upward in disdain

of town
      sweet town
           bright town
                  teeming with swarming life
like nature.

Auburn
    slender
        quick as sunlight
   I dreamed my town-dream of this fine soft her
        a future
    gentle tender loving
        open as the sky
     to the flush and fall of he and she
  and summer-skinned
              cotton-frocked fast-hearted
she set laughter in my veins
        that would evade her life
     the low broad white tight bungalow
monied preening proud
        its door shut fast against the quick of being
     the factory of her mind
the tight white bungalow in a tight white world
         property the loom and lathe
of being
so shadow fell on childhood's summer days
      grey misery of rank and class
    condemned lives for a penny's counting
      and every sweet fine trait of honest life
dismissed in favour of mismeasure's worth
     we children graded sifted
         sent through gates of failure and success
before our brains were grown
           or hearts were formed
     learning viciousness of better and of worse
        mistrusting every sweet impulse of trust
unfriendly to the pulse of friendship's drive
      schooled to shape love to mean and petty have
I outsider to the suburb creed
     glad to be unworthy in their sight
saw the brown-armed slender summer girl
               alive
               lithe
    lost to herself in the pleasure of grass
        sun

           unmeasurable joy of endless June days
                at couldn't-care-less eleven
                          and was smiled.

   And my square father had a smile
forced his face into an ugly gurn
            never in my life
               the simple gentle dawning of a look
unwilled and easy as a father's love
                  given as light
                  and darkness
as when the sun was yet to burn
                        and cold
as when the earth a frozen ball
               met me every day
            where I wanted warmth
                        a word

in fun

                  a glance
            to say love's sure
                  a touch
to set me flying into life untied
                  not pinned
      by sore bonds of sad ambition
and self-proposing property's false grin.

            Up he says
                  up
and lunacy's in my square room
                  as if a cell
      and me a bedded sorry curl
my father's big square brain
      crackling like a wireless
         his big square hands rip back the covers
               why aren't you up

      lazy

            ugly

                  tiresome boy
his big square right palm
         like a racquet swung to centre on a ball
               lands swift and perfect
on my cowed pathetic cheek.

         Town-lad
               I stood

nothing but four stone of skin and bone
        a blue-eyed crick smiled tousle-headed urchin
  still
         in the sweet rose-and-lilac garden
    in the wind-jammed autumn woods
        in the fifteen-minute-madness playground
    in the posh and snobby Grove
in the democratic street
           oh the street the yard the alley
    up from there
        up from the regimented treeless terraces
    up from the grassless backs
        up from the snug the tap-room and the lounge
    up from the dark-day factory
        up from estates as bland as bureaucrats
    up from the sullen queue for dole
        up from the bread-and-circus crowd
    up from the cold flagged scullery
           the ration book
      the deference
           up from the call-up
  lay-off lock-out pay-cut
      up from the must-do no-choice classroom
  up from the everyman idiocy of the everywhere screen
          the lounge-corner oracle
        up from the tat of Tin-Pan-Alley
the three-minute tin-eared tune
     spun to spin the wealth of boardroom spivs
        up from the unreal reel
up from newspaper witchcraft and glossy-covered voodoo
      up from the know-your-place tarradiddle
              of time-trapped parliamentarians
   up from forelock-tugging to money-puffed-up prigs
   up from delight in ignorance
       up from fear of mystifiers knowledge-hiders
          up from the terrace and the turnstile
        the money-turning turn on a tanner
     packed in for an unsporting cash-rich game
           of boodle-swerve and never lose
up from all this
       the used the abused
the exploited
         the trapped
    up from this head-against-a-brick-wall getting by
  the worked the driven the cheated the robbed

                        the polled the patronised the preached-at
                        up the townies mean-streeters
up for urban beauty and town truth
                        up for the democratic tarmac
                    kerbstone equality
            up if only not held down
                            by the sneering snotty
                        sniffy kick-the-riff-raff suburb
                the neat-lawned gulags
                        of self-exculpating excoriators
                of scroungers loafers layabouts
            confabulators conniving
        at the worthlessness of workers
        the don't-give-them-baths-to-keep-the-coal-in-brigade
            who cast a sullen ballot
        for mass misery
                    for the ugly town
            for the tight-gated ghetto of the go-getters
    and the harsh street of the hard grind of the hard-done-by.

                        I town-boy slant against the tree
            as if a wall
                    the tree outside my bayed and gabled house
                        whose lighted diamond window every day
            was like a mother's welcome to a lad
                    who in the street with bread and apple hands
                fulfilled his wish for bread and apple life
                        in street games in the one-up lovely Grove
            proles paradise
                        kids' enclosed instant
                        summer nights' sultry soaring self-loss
                            absorption in the absolute of play
                        and square-boy indoors parent-penned
                        pushed to perform in the proving universe
                            petty nothing-for-itself palaver
                                shadow life chasing shadows
                        of crass Calvinist election
                            night upon night in the tight house
                    locked in anxious misery of failure
                    miserable unloved lonely
                            life's sweet fleeting pulse
    gathered into this hard not-fail gnarl
        and gone gorgeous uncertainty's great gift
    for paltry pounds percentages and proofs
                    while I unmeasured

                except in a priceless eye-first smile
failed in every strict particular
              and rose into success unfixed
         quick and changeable as light
sure in this certainty of pride-dissolving changeability
                      street-free
     slant
           whose first life-lesson was
gutter-born
         like square-boy's first was
       better-born
           and every gesture ever since to prove it
I biting crisp sweet flesh
                 of green and juicy apple
        eyes askance for play and pull of self-escape
           square-boy chewing sun-split clay
       self-locked shrunken pride-high
           fighting every sweet and tender rush of life
         sending out before him
           this message of his proven life
         pleading to be tested
                and ever sick with wanting
to be found forever never wanting.

        From my small box's window sweet to see
           tall tennis-club trees swaying stately still
           according to the season or the day
          sweet touch of nature snobbery can't touch
            as every boy or girl has eyes for trees
a nose for summer grass and skin to love
   wood-whispering spring winds which talk of love
boys born of dads stood shoeless on hard stone
 girls mothered in sad grassless terraces
but bitter knowledge nestled my town heart
       these few who bought
              from other's strain and wrench
         a pretty plot
                 the comfort of a rose
the gentle kiss of green
     wild nature trimmed
                    and prettified
the wilderness we all once wandered in
        the strong and turgid push
   of life
         the force and throb and ache of sap

bought dear and brought to gentle this wide-spaced
   neat pleasant prissy keep-the-dross-out place
      and terraced town sucked dry of leaf and blade
as if the feet that walked there weren't the fall
         of centuries from forest-footed folk
    as if the pump and shaft and clank and whirr
         had damned love's flow for sycamore and oak
horse-chestnut and sad drooping loveliness
         of sudden winter lily-of-the-vale.

I and square-boy set at odds
                  alike in this
      unhappy love
            mother and father lost to each
and square-boy's maker injured in her pride
     rose to cold stiff absolute command
and being first he was to make the way that said
                         no shame
         and mine did likewise
            laid low by waning of a dream
      that was a child's pure absolute of love
         let bitterness confine too much her mind.

            And what a likeness to be like in
that tender sexual love
         the parent-arch a child should play beneath
               could shrivel desiccate and blow
      like dust on pavements parched by drought
         but love's a thing of time
and times that set cold pride above warm eyes
            bring power like a thug
         to club the skull of infant like
               as sweetness turns away and hides its face.

My mother had a voice that clanged one note
         a gong
      and thought of harmony as soft
or melody as waste
            and as she clanged she smiled
         so inwardly so coldly so withheld
      it turned what smiling should be inside out
            and all her clang was simple single-themed
         day by day and year by year

                  like this.

        See us see this see what we are
                see us in what we own and show
          this corner plot
this roof these floors
      oh see us moving up
    and getting on
we must get on
    all must get on who must
           and must be left behind the rest
      so I smoke *Kensington* because they're smart
          and when you hear me laugh
    ha-ha
so hard so high so tight
    you say
  now there's the laugh of someone getting on
        and what's in- born must show
come through
    shoot up
        like daffodils
    that don't appear with thorns
or petalled rose heads delicate and bright
        but grow their daffodilness
    as they must
            like us
who grow to wealth and power from our seeds
    as given as a yellow horn
  and stiff pert frost-defying stems
as in the turning of the earth there's fate
    and everything must prove itself or die
  oh there's a hurt in me might rise
        if I'm not picked
    and drown my poor mind
        and so I kick and flail and splash
  to stay somehow afloat
    and yet I drown
a thousand times a day
    at each stray thought that rises like a corpse
bloated with doubt
    to bob on the horizon
  of day mind and dark mind
      like a question
  and I won't have a question
makes my heart go jig-a-jig
        my hand reach for the packet
    light the drug that lets me suck in me

                    a twirl of smoke
a rush of poor blood-carbon to my chest
                oh for something certain sent to say
    your worth is fixed
        oh not to sleep in fear of day
in which my me is no more needed than a star
        what will I do if I'm a me reduced
                let me war against the world
oh I'd kill every living thing to keep this me of mine alive
        and we whose we was made from war
                must war
            against that we that's made of something else
                see them
see them going every day to school
                hair like rats' tails
        low kind
                cheap kind
        made for the estate
                the till
the town
oh give me arms'll keep the low where they belong
        it must be written in the skies
                that I was made for better
they for worse
    it must be granted in the turning of the earth
ordered in Pluto's origins
                fixed in furthest reaches of infinity
    that I am chosen
                they denied
for should it be that chance has brought me here
        should it be my me is no more final than a flea
        should it be creation holds no proof
                of my more worth
then all my mind's a flimsy tower of straws.

I square-boy raised in this
            my mind was all it-must-be and I prove
a mind so frozen to its own sweet prompt
            that only unkind thoughts
        and cruel stabs
and scrabbling grasping sharp-nailed need
        to set a me as rigid as cement
        spoke to that me who lived in light
the voices of a mind denied
            yet so the dawn and dusk of all my thought

        my thought was nature made them so
                and as my mind was set like this
            so my thought said so all minds must be set
and so they were
            in this fine place
    upon its hill
        the town below
the dirty river snaking out to sea
            one bank urban
        un-urbaned the other
        the universe a sorting-house for human worth
except that funny little town-boy mind
        this creature quick and natured as a wren
            exception in his limbs and looks and laugh
      make me odd moments question
my high tight knot of pride
    and certainty to out-endure the sun.

    Town-boy I read the utter otherness of stars
      and felt my soft self melt
        oh delicious me that's just a thing of moments
          not given for millennia like light
          like stars
        but shifting with a minute's difference
          soaring on a smile
      cast down by cold closed lids
          a taut averted face
      electric thousandth-second flick of life
            quick with every change
            of look or pose or tone
      this ever-changeful bless of being
            not the thoughtless fixity of moons.

Pre-fab age
our neat brick school was pre-fabbed at its edge
    one east one west
        and here I came square-boy on the bright days
        and the rainy days
        on the cold mornings and the dull mornings
            here I came to learn
        because decided boys must learn
            and girls
                in neat brick buildings
                pre-fabs
            quick erections not to last

                    standing for decades
                              miraculous erections
                    and here was childhood
enclave of learning
                    these little people set aside to read
        and add
    the adult world a world away
                    and happiness a quiet room
                              friends
        story
                              balsa-wood bi-plane
                    cricket bat smell of grass
                    curtained Friday-afternoon film hall
                              and here I came unhappy
            to drink the State's free daily milk
                and fill my brain with what the State ordained
                    my State-hating parents at my back with
                              get on and prove yourself
                    prove yourself in the State school
                              so we who hate the helping State
                    and love the warring State
                              can by your proof be proven
so here I worked and worked
            and hated work
                    hating myself for working
                              and hating work
                    working for proof that never came
        dog-and-its-tail game
                    and learnt hard sums big words
            and scripture
    and how to give answers that gave marks
            in the crowded quiet room
        with a kindly teacher telling how
        or a cruel teacher making pain
I worked out when the trains would pass
            if one leaving London at eleven
        steamed north at fifty
and another quitting Manchester at ten
            chugged south at sixty
        and distance speed and time
were all in bed with one another
            when would the climax come
        I conned the names of capitals and kings
        and knew that plants had stigma-stamen sex
        and rank promiscuous bees

like drunken youths
        drank from every offered mouth
     to fill the world with flowers
    and yet no flowers grew within my life
       and days passed in a pause
    as if some day days would begin
but didn't.

          Young flowers
   beautiful and tender
     nodding lovely heads on gracious stems
   blonde or auburn flowers
        what an education then I gleaned
   from their quick eyes
and smiles as swift as swallows
    what brain-fire couldn't flash
  from camera-click two-second glance
   and what was other learning next to this
an eyelid's flick the flash of happiness.

          But my square brain was all for proof
       oh passing looks were far too here-and-gone
          to ground a worth that's fixed
       young flowers passed me by
      and that sweet heart-flame
          licking out of nought
         lay in my brain a mere pulsing cinder
    unblown by kindling breath
          that needs pursed lips
       and died.

          Young brains
   the future's clay
     and in huge London
         far away
        unknown
  important men were fixing ways
  to weigh intelligence
        new bump-feelers looking for
the big heads and the small heads
    the brains endowed by nature to be those
        of leaders lucre-lovers lie-peddlers
   the brains deprived by nature to be those
of labour losers led-by-the-nosers
       so into our small minds

             the minds of children
                     minds made by the making of together
                         fell the fell idea
              of impregnation's fateful instant
or the sudden rising of a streak that said
                    succeed or fail
            as if before the boiling earth had cooled
                   or water run in tiny rivulets
             where once cascades of lava rolled unchecked
                    some pre-existent sense
some nowhere mind
              had pre-ordained the ledger of our lives.

                    Ah kindliness
              that primrose spared amongst the weeds
how does it bloom against the strangling vice
        of thrusting thistles
and luck dropped on us
        in our final year
        a sweet kind man who made our class
a little world of pleasure and of light
        and all we learned we learned as one
and sank back into friendship like a bed
        that bears you up and turns your tiredness glad
        so day comes singing through your limbs
    and lifts you up from weariness to play.

        Here teacher in my tweed and tie
State sanctioned to grade minds to set
        the chosen on their paths to wealth and place
the others to tread stony ways to shame
        a shifting shiftless system made
        to shaft the weak unworthy or too sweet
            and I who liked a child to be a child
            loved the quick intelligence of smiles
and lifted high my high-achievers
        the excellent the out-ahead
        in friendship kindness tolerance and grace
    the vicious tightness of the bitter fight for worth
            curare in my heart
        finding fear a dunce's cap and corner
tried to make my classroom light with love of life
            and stories making painting
        building playing finding
        filled the days of these

              who I hoped lucky
          kept tests and measurements at bay
and strived to let them learn
         without the tear of pass or fail
    the adult world at bay
        and cash
the pimp that drags down to its own vile tank
        of septic festered stinking faecal rank
           all beauty joy and truth
        was cast away so this clean clever place
    could be a haven for these tender brains.

What good was that to me
a woman injured in her pride will fight
    the sky itself
        and injury is everywhere
when worth admits the few
            and damns the rest
      I'll have him up among the best
like these my neighbours with their fate-touched sons
          two brains to win them
        place and power and worth
    reward for nature's chance
            the petty firing of our brains' soft cells
    and this
        this freak this blip
this sliver of a difference
      imperfection of the species' haul
    from stark survival in the midst of mystery
        to this
      the use of elbows knees and knives
to carve a quaver's distance that sounds safe
      asylum in the money-jungle
      evidence beyond all doubt
            of place
    what good to me he's kindly to my child
if kindliness means failure
        what good a happy child without the means
    to cut a way to better
        happiness
            a creed for fools
    I'd rather see my children miserable and rich
than blithe and cast aside
      what's misery
  a petty price for power

> and misery's a gain
> when others' lives hang on your word or act
> then who is happy
> send happy to the dogs
> let snarling viciousness rip happy brain to gut
> some other place and time was made for that
> my trap is climb or fail
> and who will love us if we fall.

        I went on
day to day
        just going on
        husband to this clothes-line Cleopatra
            this anthracite Xanthippe
father to this unloved brood
        my love left elsewhere
    this my going on
        my what-I-must
    just keeping going
        small things felt like mine
    a pipe
        a pint
    odd days the paper
sometimes work
    a sudden sense it might all be worthwhile
  this selling
    these false smiles
this mouthing better than it is
    only to collapse at six
        like me
    my big frame crumpled in a chair
in my smart spotless living-room
        with love elsewhere
    from she I never heard of
        somewhere in the world
    her smile
her hair
    those reddish lights
        the way she wore it in a tail
    and how it fell
one strand across her brow
    and how she smiled
    that big white smile
        her voice a kindness
    when she said the most banal of things.

        Love as ordinary as rain
has swept out like a storm
            this quiet devastation in its wake
    the haunting of my waking days
and hate as ordinary as rain
            sits still and milky like this northern sky
  I walk beneath
        a man who was a man
      no she to make me
                 just this unsexed hurt
        a viper vigilant in its pride
as loving as a snake
    and that sweet pulse once lifted me from me
    deserts me into death
  my only destination out of dead man's life
        the flat one-noted still unshifting realm
    where what I call my life
must ebb away

        like sewage in a drain.

Two schools
    one ancient private-founded out of wealth
  the other modern paid for by that hand
    that takes from what is public made
and public makes
    like a gift
        of apples
    to the she whose garden bounds the tree
        and out of every hundred
twenty only to the first
        every eighty failed
               at sweet eleven
    neat Nazism of mild-mannered Mengeles
        read our bumps by scientific means
and sorted us
    like blue eyes brown eyes thin or fat
  fair/dark
    all privilege to one all shame upon the rest
and something in our monkey minds
    clicks on at any sign of edge
        an atavistic aching for a lead
    some good response to sweetness and to smiles
that makes us swell with pride
    when turned to cold selection by an art

as black as witchcraft
	false as power's tongue
		turned twenty against eighty
	as if some blight was in the most.

   And how was I to go town-boy as I was
      through a Latined gate with lads
   whose pride was out of town ?

   And how was I to go square-boy as I was
   along the failures' lane
   when all the family-making of my mind
   said failure is the worst
   		of all the world's harsh worsts ?

And so I went one careless early day
	to meet a fate laid out as if by fate
   and what I found
		was something made me laugh
	this foolish man-made mess
of discipline and force and grades and streams
		a mania for measuring
	as if a poor lunatic let loose
had framed a system meant to be
		the mirror of his own short mind.

And so I went one anxious early day
   to find a fate laid out no doubt by fate
  and what I found
		was something pricked me preen
	this cut-aboveness made
of discipline and force and grades and streams
		a miracle of measuring
	as if the universe's genius let loose
had framed a system meant to be
	the spit of nature's lifting of the few.

		My luck was grass and woods
	fresh air big space
girls as full of love as lanes in spring
		warm friends
	and town
that place I came from
			common as a smile
				and called me back

      because the hub of all our common life
and oh how gladly common amongst these
    the failures
even in a suburb stiff as ice
      as common as a daisy or a fly
  to buzz and flower common like the air
or trees
    common as an after-dinner sleep
and flourishing among all common things
      it made no sense to set a razor's width
between a mind could con equations' knack
    or turn a tense in ten languages at once
and those who couldn't plot the fall of x
      or sift a past anterior from rice
    for all that's common drew these minds in close
  much more than bits of learning forced apart
    and who but madmen preen at nature's gift
    making much of what they've little earned.

              Demented
manic loony nuts off-the-wall plain barking
      everything explained
  in this world which opens to explaining
      like slate to rain
not science which must stand aside from what it knows
    but ignorance as knowing as in
  seven days to make a world
      and two by two in floods
  not stories any more but truths
        to whip a mind to madness
and from all this how sweet to lapse
to make a me that meets the world without
      an explanation meant to say
    all that is is as it is because it must be so
    leave me sweet accident like this
  my raincoat loop catching the gate latch
    as I run in between the posts
    a hook I couldn't make
  that happens as it happens by a fluke
  so million-to-one it shouts aloud
    this world that threw us up
  is cast of chance and all we are not had-to-be
but this because not other
    then what a miracle is she to me
      an accident of eyes and hair and hands

a wonderment of glances and of smiles
               I'm expert in her voice's syllabus
     top-streamed for reading of her sighs
head-boy in hearing every subtle note
     of love's unspoken music in her words
school's unintended lessons I soak up
         a blotting paper for the ink of her
   and loafing through the day's mad push for grades
     work flat-out on the language of her look
and this it is makes Crow Hill's Road alive
           and Crookings Lane a path to paradise
and down Church Ave and through the bluebell wood
    where bare-kneed climbing sliding muddied stung
 was boyish happiness
         I walk my limber way to town she in my head
    over dirty Ribble where the ships arrive
      the big world shrunk to fit my little home
  hammer and sickle   maple leaf
  and I a boy amazed at all their size
       and what they brought and why
and who they were
     stride now half-manly on the arc-spined bridge
         thigh up the hill to Fishergate   my town
    and Cheapside Friargate Main Sprit Weind
      belong to me as everyone
 the democratic anarchistic streets
    in spite of ownership
the feeling town ignites will not be owned
 and in that spark there lives the impish flame of a reborn world
   that needs the kindling breath of many
to set alight in every mind
     a fire to cauterize the sickened nerve of fear
and set in place in place of that in this hurt place
    the free and open world of all for all.

      Closed
against the poor the dim the down the dross
           closed the door I passed through
    shut against the many so that we
the few who merit passage uplift gain
     can have our place
     and keep them fixed in theirs
        closed
my mind against itself
        sometimes those soft sweet pulsings

        and town-boy unlike me
            his whisper of a smile aflame for girls
and fearless of the loss that grips my brain
            in fear
        he goes at life and mocks at death itself
        and I am lost to know his carelessness
            borne up by a creed that crushes me
pushing to be special chosen first
        and if not first at least in that per cent
    where failure is a word we never hear
            if I could find a thing outside myself
        to take me out of me
but oh I fall back ever into fear
            of being less than all
        and nothing that I do is ever real
but everything a game to show some force
        beyond me and above me I'm worthwhile
        every tick and mark cries out I'm real
and through this narrow gate where I must squeeze
        the rest shan't come
their falling is my rising
        they must fail
or else what yardstick measures my success
    is there a unit absolute of merit
is it written in the stars I'm picked
        did nature knead my brain to be elite
            then let their second-rateness be on show
deny them access money power say
        put stigma on them let them know they're less
            how else to show that I surpass them all
    failure's my creed for others
        so may election shine
and yet I'm dimmed among these ball-mad boys
            by clumsiness and no sense for a bounce
and even where I should catch all the light
        another's shadows cuts
and I'm not first in anything
        least of all my parents' love
my cold and inward mother shuts me out
        as I must shut out all that isn't me
    sucks on her succouring cigarettes
            and shrouded in her narcissistic smoke
    her nicotined dark dim narcotic den
        denies the real of me and all I need
because the real of her is lost
        like smoke that drifts up grey and thin and slow

                to lose itself in air   inches from the ceiling's height
           so she all upward all her real pushed down
is gathered in this rarefied thin space
                where all she breathes is her
          and there's no room for me   nor him
my father sharing her cold bed
      demeaned enraged he takes revenge on me
vicious-voiced mad-faced fixed-eyed
              he comes at me with murder meant for her
           who's murdered him with coldness
          and even when no bruises mark my flesh
I'm dead within   except for this one wish to be in front
   unlike exception   noticed for my else
        I pick each small eccentric tic of mind
     and push it to its limit to cry   me
and this sad trick is all I call my life   and town
        that place of many
I despise
     I hate the streets that any feet can walk
         crave exclusion
fences gates locks wire
     I loathe the bus that carries human dross
I scorn what's public   shared   what all can know
       I want estates I dream of power and land
    I want keep out emblazoned on my heart
I want a me so big it is the world
        no separation set to cast me out and down
    so small I can be lost
     I want to build a fortress out of wealth
   wall out each debt of friendship or of love
I want a me that's absolute not you alloyed
     so what are girls to me
           except the cold excitement of a lust
the rubbing off of unaffectioned need
    This other I won't have
        for other means my me is less than all
   and all that's less is less than I require
   to keep my mind from spinning off its hub
     and down into that messy pit I fear
   of thick untutored never nurtured need
      which might dispatch me back to all I was
when her tight fissure dumped me in the world
    a lump of flesh whose mind she couldn't make.

    Strange to me this place because I come from streets
   and streets have made my mind

             because I know the harsh shared backs
                without a flower or tree or blade
             strange and wonderful the loveliness of lilac
        the dense resisting privet neatly clipped
             strange and sweet the roses and hydrangea
        the sparrows blackbirds starlings blue-tits wrens
                      strange to be a stranger in your home
                   how memory of what I've never known
                                has cast the mould of me
           and how my heart harks when I hear
                Keir and Nye and Tillett Mann and Foot
                   for it's a thing of hearts
        arithmetic as simple as a child's
                   calls out its truth
             this one percent that sits atop the pile
        and eats its fill
             while twenty at the bottom grinds and scrapes
        a truth so simple must be hid by lies
             that sicken hearts make limbs weigh lead
           brains spin to pull this out-of-kilter frame
             back into focus makes the heartbeat sweet
                   and I who'd scoot off into happy life
             am held by this
                   that cold injustice marked me for unworthy
        and could I choose a life I wouldn't choose
                to have to fight to lift this crushing stone
                   but not to fight would be to live their lie
        so I'm condemned to fight or live in death.

                But strange to live among those I must fight
                      such friends
                   who hate a terrace
                            scorn hard hands
                   whose minds were made by avenues and groves
                      whose little edge of comfort is enough
        to light up fear of falling
             to find in semi garage garden drive
                   distinction   might set species well apart
        while I find in an ocean's span of wealth
                      no human sign
                and how my time denies my very fate
                   says on life's playing board each chancer falls
           into the square his talents drew him for
                   and makes us lie and trim.

                                                              37

                Him
        that loose town-boy
                he's all hims to me
                      who lifts me from myself and makes me his
though I'm not yet and fear I'll never be
                he's bliss and torment in one lovely frame
        dream of possession nightmare I might lose
all I could want and all I fear to have
        for having
        would I be cut out to keep
                a boy like that
    a drug to female brains
                      and being so I want so yet so fear
        so if I could I wouldn't
                but I might
and there I am by calculated chance
just where I know he'll be and might yet ask
and sometimes all my future seems a path
        as clear and straight and blue as his bright gaze
as friendly as his crooked-corner smile
                as if I laid down since light first quit the sun
        and sometimes every thought of him brings pain.

But I've a father fills up half my mind
        and town-boy's all he'd have me never have
too loose too easy
        lacking in the pride
that's all that keeps my father's mind afloat
        and mine
        made out of music he composed
needs too that upward flight to set me free
                yet how I'm pinned by what I try to flee
and this warm love that fills my veins with peace
        can turn to vicious hate at a thought's jolt
                as if this me that loves
    is someone else
as if this me that hates is what I am
        yet when I see his eyes the love is me
  so how this hate that takes me for its own
        and how to have a me that feels like mine
    while he's composed of streets I've never known
                my feeling formed to fit suburban spite
  I love him yet I hate all he comes from
he's money-glib cares nothing for a suit
        and this sweet easiness I find so kind
  is madness folly set by all I've learnt

                    of each for each and all at war with all
                if we are made to fight and strive for gain
what kind of creature gives away his edge
                    two mes I have that war and won't retreat
    this I that's soft and tender can't resist
        this me that's made for status can't relent
            a boy like him should earn my straight contempt
        ambition doesn't drive him to exceed
            he's happy to appear less than he is
yet all my parents' teaching melts and fails
when he creates a world they've never told
            from nothing but a glance a smile a word
                and which is true
my mind won't let me know
            and day by day I'm torn and thrown about
            one moment sweet the next black widow sharp
                    hoping in turn he'll turn sharp as I am
                and grant my hate a freeing full excuse.

    I suck my *Kensington* in the sweet sun
fenced in
        my garden trimmed like minted notes
                my glasses hide my eyes
    but I can see
and look out on a world that makes me fear
        those down the hill who sun in tight brick backs
    but have a cross like me to shape the world
            and won't their gutter-envy make them want
        a garden just like mine
                a space
                        a fence
but if all have as much as me
                            I've less
            I've only more if some must be deprived
                so it must be that my more is deserved
or else their less is simple cruel deceit
        yet those with less are more
                and they can cross
a paper to elect who'd slice off mine
    to lift them
            drag me down
                    oh monstrous creed
        that sets the natural order on its head
                    for it must be
throughout all human time
            that we the few have more because we should

                my brain spins
        and my heart kicks on my ribs
                to think that they can vote to change the world
                that we have shaped to safety for ourselves.

That man who doesn't love me earns my bread
and dreams of loving elsewhere like a fool
        but I've him boxed and fettered like a bull
emasculated by my tongue that won't
        explore his mouth or lick his manhood limp
I'm trapped he's trapped
                        that's two entrapped as one
                I hate him straight and would walk out today
                        except for these
        my garden house and place
                without him I'd be down the hill amongst
                the terraced many whose advance I dread
                but how my woman's heart cries out against
                        the parting of my flesh by his hard hate
what cruelty's in nature that it makes
        the flesh rise up when all affection's dead
                his body that I hate more than his mind
                        lies heavy on me thrusting sweaty mad
to rub off all its tension where I'm warm
                and wet and hot and tight and meant for love
                how I long for dryness
                        then he'll know hurt
        when he drives hard his ageing passion home
                and though I hate that these things live conjoined
which ought to fight like poles that won't be touched
                warm love cold money twine around my mind
                        I'll love his wallet though I hate his heart.

                        Now
who comes to my garden but town-boy
        my eldest's erstwhile pal when play was all
and those blue eyes remind me of my loss
                what woman wouldn't love a boy like this
what wife not want a husband so possessed
        his mother's age I'll almost flirt with him
                my flesh exposed to catch the peaking sun
        and yet he comes from those
                        who I despise
        the backstreet mass that swarms and feels its day
        is come
                and all it has to do is wait

            to have four bedrooms garage and a lawn
he comes from those I scorn and yet he's sweet
enough almost to make me say their lives
            are worth as much as ours
     and yet I won't
   exception is exception
               let it stand
     he's almost one of us except his way
is too street easy friendly come-what-may
            he treats his chances as a passing wind
   won't fight and grab and push and strive for place
and still I wish my son had more of him
      such manners
            natural
                 unforced
   fresh as dew.

Some few like him to move up from their rows
       and be like us
   why can't we stop at that
but change that might be wrought when millions move
    and might move then not some from low to high
        but holus-bolus shift us to new ways
oh no that must be fought to very death
      else we are doomed to lose not only this
   our gardens hedges houses kitchens cars
    which outclass theirs in money airs and style
     but self itself for all we are is made
     from these small differences in property
      I'm me because not them they're them
    because paid less heard less
         less meant-to-be
and some way must be found to halt their march
      some freedom-looking trick to keep us safe
   a suburb creed to keep the town at bay
      say merit lets you in
    or keeps you out
   their place is fixed
       our elevation saved.

All I could want for love's demand and yet
     sweet girl
       what's got your mind set at self odds
       the town in me the street my nothing lost
   when nothing's your inheritance and all's
     to win

                together
                        not that hapless scam
                that holds the narrow gate ajar for one
                        shuts on the rest
                        and rolls out razor wire
                                of meritless
                        unworthy
                        cut below
            no none of that's for me it's true I throw
my chances to the wind in that false race
            I won't be measured
        all the life I own
    is what's together made
                        my me made so
        for if I stand alone where is my mind
and yet alone I stand
                once common made
            and you uncommon in each lovely fact
of hair and eyes and poise and voice and tone
                why fear what made us
            fear sets us apart
why drag a heavy burden through the world
                it's accident that makes our quick hearts beat
                        sets our twinned brains alight
                        why not relax
 it's fine to be as light as swooping swifts
                we must be what we are
and though you've grown
                    in suburbs money snobbery and pride
            it's nothing but a phase
                        our life's a blip
our tenancy's been long these things are short
        and what are we in life's great onward march
            the best we ever do is to kiss life
    full on the mouth
        as I'd kiss you if you'd
                be kissed by lips that won't lisp to the lies
        that turn a penny's difference into scales
            set up to weigh our human worth like meat
                we'll all be minced by idiocies like that
            your mind can change for minds are only made
        of making up our minds to live one way
                and though our choice's limits are hard fixed
within there's almost endlessness of choice
        for every nanoshift in making life
        fires newness in our brains that makes us new

                    sweet girl
            see change as freedom
                    learn to laugh
at fixity that fears how we are cast
        by nature to be changed by what we change
            I'm town-made
that's my nature
                I've a mind
    that loves a street as much as fields and oaks
the towns we've made have made us
            that's our fate
        we're urban
            those mean streets are who we are
        if we're to blend
            me minded for the town
        you for the gate the garden and the hedge
whose fences must come down
        who needs to rise
    sweet girl
            let's meet in woods and kiss like streets.

The misery of days in which I wait
for promised days of life no more postponed
and work to win approval never comes
so all that's left is clinging to this pride
of better
not like them
admitted

safe

yet my small cold and lonely loveless room
in this square house love never entered holds
no promise of the warm embrace I crave
acceptance
access
false no more
arrived
my life's a journey to a land I lost
when my cold mother spread her lying thighs
and my hard father used her cleft to win
mere respite from the mocking pulse of lust

and out of this harsh coupling came a boy
unloved
unneeded

       welcome as a curse
          oh heartless nature that can make us breed
more flesh than love
     and how was I to make
   myself a self to meet the selves I'd meet
    when self is made by scanning other selves

            far in the inward nothings dotting space
is emptiness that once was something bright
     like them I've lost my centre
           fallen dark
and anti-life sucks all my striving down
    my infant eyes that searched
        for signs of love
found nothing but black holes of self-intent
          the breast on which I lay my head was cold
      and gentle voices never summoned sleep
         one cold reply came sure to all my pleas
           to prove
                to not let down

   to stonewall shame
and it must be as earth's held by the sun
     if shame cannot be ours it must be theirs
    if I'm to be borne up some must go down
   this is the creed I sucked at her cruel breast
    and my one comfort in this aching void
is some are less than me
        more hurt
        more spurned
    the poor the weak the failed deserve my scorn
   my eyes seek out the rich
        the proud
           the harsh

I'll bow to them I'll fawn
   I'll stoop to rise
    for when I see myself like them I feel
exempt from all my hurt
         admitted
           home
   as if I'd had a mother held me close
and loved me for my imperfection's blaze
     as imperfection is our human mark
     and shame a spur that's set to make us ride
  at speed when we feel we might slip and fall
   but we've made shame a whip to lash the poor
and we who rise above

        wipe out its mark
        and wear instead this ribbon of high pride
bright badge of property
        fair won by brains
yet I'd use vile foul means to keep me up
        for I've my parents show me foul ways
who speaks of justice
    fairness
tush
              to hell
                they're words I'll use
                when things go well for me
who says I'm hard to others mard to self
    I know no other way
           my mind is set
        to hurt those who fall short
        so I might rise
             and rise I must

                    or in my falling die.

If I'd been born for fields woods and streams
my mind would sing with those
        and love a track
  and love them yet I do like anyone
the touch of bark a turgid leaf the smell
        of rainy autumn or the cuff of wind
  that hits you on a hill's peak
                cuts your breath
        but these just aren't my fate
no mind-song's here
    to call to me like tarmac brick and glass
    a new song's to be learnt from gutters up
        and I born close to gutters can't renege
    what home is this to me
that won't admit
    the makers of my flesh and mind

                        my breed
    except in ones or twos when they've cast off
        the mark of all that made them
                snapped the bond
    of making life together all for all
        sweet girl
must this turn sour for nothing's sake
        except more bricks and mortar
           drives and grass

what's made is made
    but making's yet to come
let's laugh at gone before seize what's to be
    shall we drag yesterday
            like Pharoah's stones
into tomorrow we've a right to make
    shall we be cut asunder by
            what's gone
what is this madness drags us from our bliss
    this time's not ours
                    we came into a world
    full formed before the cells that made us split
            why then permit a time we didn't make
                            make us

is all we are the playthings
                    of the age
    and life a strutting farce of parts
    we mouth and never make our words our own
    is all that's dead to weigh on us like fate
our lives to be entrapped in brick and coin
            what's old can live if life's what made it sing
        let's make a freshness takes what's best of old
  let honeysuckle grow by every door
let's work to make a pleasantness for all
        what holds you's only thinking this is meant
                and can't be other like the sun must swell
    to burn and spit out all we love as ash
        but there's no meaning in a glance or touch
save what we grant
            our meaning's made
                        not fixed

        like   quantity
don't let them tie you to
            a figure
        pin you with percentages
for then your mind's cash-chaosed into loss.

            There's hate in me I hate and want dispelled
but won't dissolve while sniffiness sits fine
            upon its prissy hill and sneers at town
        and then there's love
            sweet girl
                    mind's better pulse
        and laughter
                lovely solvent of thick pride
                    but it's a thing of moments

                once it's made
a choice sits like an engine on its tracks
and runs the same fixed narrow route for years
                till points are switched
            then let love oil the wheels
    let's make our journey pleasure every day
                    we two
        against the world
                we two
                    for all.

And when my children grew
            and turned and left
    so left with only her and she with me
what were we left with
            but the leavings of
    the sorry meal of marriage's cold fare
            some small mistake of thinking put me here
                an instant
                in a young man's easy mind
which can't conceive such loneliness or pain
    made me ignore the voice that said get out
some hardness in her
                peeled my straining nerves
        and yet I let it go and her to make
a niche within me that would fill with bile
        and poison every sickening weary cell
for years
            because of one quick moment when
                the choice before me
        yes or no
                    like that
    computer tight
                I failed
                        relaxed
        let go
    the staying courage could have kept me safe
descending to the time's low silly grade
            of let it be
                and it'll do
                    who cares
because so lonely unattached afraid
        of never finding fatherhood and love
    a desperate fool I let her play her tricks
of loving woman gentle to my needs
        five-minute legerdemain of female skill

to reel me in and pin me
　　　　　　　　　fixed and dead
　　　　　and hate of her made hateful what we bred
　　　　　　　was I a father
　or a man who came
　　　　　and went
　　　　　　　　　with money in his wallet for
　　　the building of a fortress of fine things
　　　　　to hide the hovel where our hearts all died
　　　　　an ant that carries on its back more weight
than flexing human strength could ever shift
　　　　　was not more borne with carrying
　　　　　　　　　　　　　　　　　　than me

　and blind in all it does
　　　　　does all with all
　　not lonely abject empty self-disdained
　　　rejected in his manhood wounded cursed
and everything that lives has one short life
　　　and that life shortened in its range and pitch
　ends sooner than its end
　　　　　　　　　and all that's left
　　regret and pain
　　　　　　　　　the past you could have made
　　a tender set of memories for old age.

I can't
**　　I'm stalled**
**　　although I know it's right**
**　　　I think it's wrong**
**　　my mind rides on the tides**
I need to fix on voices I've grown with
**　　　　　　　and you**
**　　you beckon to a twig you climb**
**　　　　you risk your limber limbs and scoff at breaks**
**　　　　　　but I'm not made to throw away a lead**
**　　　　those little bits of money you disdain**
are life and death to us who live by gaps
**　　　　and horrified by what you think is fun**
**　　　the way you tug the edge of our day's rug**
to make the person-order somersault
**　　　what can I do but close my door against**
**　　the me I am when you smile mischief's lure.**

　　　　　　Sweet girl
the world's not flat

        square-boy the sun
sits still
        what grips our minds as truth is false
as spin
 and change comes hard because we hold
        our being in a cup that fills and brims
        and fear each tiny nudge each petty spill
        so every fact that makes a drop displace
            brings dread as if the sky's about to fall
            and we deny the earth's a crooked ball
or say the sun shifts as it seems to do
            or can't believe we crawled out of the sea
            nor see that money's measure's all a sham
but I've a mind that makes me want to laugh
            at all that's set as sure
      including me
what's false denies and gives us cockroach brains
        what's true we'll never know
what's skewed we can.

        I'm townward for its truth
   there's no mind else
      we don't debate on hills
     decide in woods
and liquid streets are solvents of hard pride
  a king's unknown who walks with tarmac's mass.

      Here's love
         sweet girl
and friendship too square-boy
        free offered without let or power's twist
but love and friendship flourish where no step
        trips up approach or sets too high a bound.

      A stranger here
          among the lawns and groves
      at home with lawns
        and pleased with space and spare
        I'd never settle into this hedged life
            here nothing wants to move
      except get slick
as if one half our brains is jammed and spins
  and mind can't find its way from its own maze
but when I heard feet march and saw the crowd
  heard tools go down and gates click strictly shut

                saw justice raise her face
         like a young girl
            towards the sunlight innocent unlearned
that beauty always rouses ugliness
            sweet tenderness calls viciousness to life
    each smile sets envy's nerve alive in some
            each private joy brings murder to its feet
    a gentle whispered word elicits spite
and love which pulls an inch above the norm
    awakens hatred never shuts its eyes
            what's given freely sets free greed's delight
    cool modesty makes pride climb on its back
    the hand unclenched invokes the fist made tight
            the selfless act brings running selfish hordes
        the unarmed self invites the sharpened blade
            I knew that every vileness known on earth
was not enough to keep me from her cause
    because I'm friendly with wet slate rough bricks
drainpipes gutters kerbstones chimney-stacks
    give me the clematis climbs taut cement
                so I must stand for this
    we're made by town
                nor let the cold erection of stiff pride
            rape fresh democracy's warm noble flesh
I rush to streets where all are on a par
            and every offer's every offer's thanks
once stiff election's myth's laughed off its plinth
    there's kindness in the tarmac's flattened face
    no Calvin on street corners where we meet.

        Where's rank today
            what's petty place to us
        there's early morning odour of fresh ground
            and rousing for the day's new waiting work
        in this primeval-modern place we've made
            like nature makes all newness bottom up
                executive a word unknown
                    to stars
        to rocks and mountains deserts ice-caps streams
            to rivers grasses mosses monkeys
    men
            except when high on saving arrogance
        that blind self-fooling flight that mars our minds
            some brain-trick wired in to lift us from
humiliation's devil makes us weak

        unsuited to stand up to life's tough tasks
with patchwork layered brains made bit by bit
through time so long and lost we gasp to think
      we are its petty heirs
          and all we're part of makeshift
a cobbled nature fitted to survive
conditions made before our making's march
    and made by nature's making
            we then made
our natures from the gift of nature's grant
  queer natured to make whole what nature gives
town's not just ours is what we've made ourselves
     and by the square's horse chestnut
near the road
       my quiet print and coffee corner close
            I'm home
and home for all of us is here
  the broad and equal street
     a home for each.

If I had all the world or if my self
could reach the universe's farthest edge
  still all that lies beyond me would raise fear
I'll not be separate but will blend so all
  creation's where I am and I am all
 and all I share this planet with unreal
  this man
    my intimate my rutting mate
      I'll be as cold to him as if a corpse
  the nights I've stiffened at his stiffened want
should I be warm
     inviting
         should I fold
should I be me through him then I'll depend
    so I'm a board
      a stone made for his hurt
he'll rub against me till his nerves bleed pain
  for all that I can maim is in my grip
 whatever lives beyond me's dead to me
   what way to know that I'm alive but this
that you will suffer if you suffer me
      I'm sharp abrupt my being is a rasp
  whatever lifts beyond itself I hate
        I'll be hard-centred or I'll cease to be
death's better than a life of high demands
that risk a me can hurt when others fail

I'll push into the world this me that claims
it's worth through owning pushing
                getting on
we few who get and set the rest a task
      whose setting makes their failure sure as light
      and who makes these
  the things that make me me
    who laid these bricks joined wood
                    fixed pipe to pipe
crawled under boards to clip the cables tight
nailed slates hauled gutters
              painted boards and spouts
who wove this carpet only best feet walk
who smoothed the plaster on my walls that keep
    the quick and handy dirty-handed out
who turned the part and fixed the parts that churn
    who worked the weary line to make the car
      whose polished surface
              gleams to show our worth
         who digs the street to give me light and heat
who baked the bread
    who drove the early van
why should I care
    these things are mine not theirs
and let them earn
    so long as we earn more
and let them rise
    so long as ones and twos
        but I would kill the street if I had means
and gate this enclave
  set the snarling dog
  keep town where it belongs
      low
          poor
              and cramped
    its heart alone a rich commercial pool
where I may fish for trinkets rare and dear
    what else is me
unhappy in my man
my mothering all pain of will they shine
      oh how I hate that public joining scheme
  to take down brick by brick
              wealth's proving wall
and lay a flat arena all can walk
  they'd close the pathway off
             that leads up here

          and no-one to look down on
how could I
      endure to look straight-sighted at myself
I crave a private space that gives me bounds
                who owns a school
the beds the sick lie in
      and if I'm what I am by what I own
what's owned by all's subtraction from my me
      that door where all can enter shuts me out
when I can shut another in the cold

                        I'm real
and who will call that cruel
   I'm kind
will pat a dog
         give pennies to the blind
but what's an act of kindness won't enhance
      my self
             who shines for open acts
all life's a test and I must pass or fail
    I'll garner points to set me one above
and surely kindness keeps them in their place
    it's mad outrageous vicious false to sense
to set them higher than their grant permits
             each one a place
   determined by their gift
that's law laid down by nature
        out of time
all things must have an order strictly fixed
     and money's measure lets us see our worth
that else is hidden
      oh sweet trick of coin
how I give thanks that this gives me a means
    to prove what else
          slides free from grasp of proof
   the happy day when we could say this much
of gold makes me
      this much more worth than you
marks when our life began
      before we were

                    just apes
let's not think origins so lost
   I'll live in narrow lines our time has drawn
because they raise me by a precious inch
   and that small space is all I know of life.

        And all I know of life is limping loss
            this empty house my aching tomb
we two
        like sorry corpses that the wind makes talk
this dumb-show staged
    to fool ourselves we're real
a spectacle to blind believing eyes
        and yet that's something
loveless broken dry
    I've house and car and hedge
            and gate and notes
  to keep me up
    them low as it should be
      we're one in that
          our marriage there holds firm
what's left to me of life shall stand for this
    that measured
        I've the measure of most men
    count percentages
      do ranking sums
  most fools shall fall below me I'm amongst
    those few who count for something in my time
           and bitter though this consolation is
       what else
          if there's a life but this I'm lost
I'll not think that I'm nothing but a blip
    creation's tiny nothing lost in time
      my poor heart strains to fly out of my chest
    when mind reminds me how
            I'm here and gone
      oh what can hold it
    who can keep me sane
        when all life's set to be a final proof
and proof proves fleeting as a sparrow's song
    then cling to money
        say amount's the same
    as quality
      so I've a vessel holds
  against the roaring mouths of lion waves
    that cast me on a fluxing sea and say
  all's change
        no instant's ever twice
          all life
is movement
    nothing's fixed no proof

        exists
            of worth when worth's
                    as hard to grasp as light
            for who can stand outside his petty frame
and measure others on some perfect scale
  who's god to claim perspective outside time
      who sees with other than a human eye
      such thoughts can melt my mind
           leave me adrift
                I've shut them out
  say is and must are one
what's gone is dead
      what's yet to come who cares
I'll make my time all time because it serves
  and kill each thought that says my time's a lie
      and so wish death
                        on everyone who speaks
the thoughts my own mind won't admit
                or die.

      Call me sweet girl once more then let me go
          your eyes won't see these eyes again
              these lips
          you'll never hear my voice nor I light up
                at yours
          there's something holds me from your charm
      as if I'd rather poison than fresh food
      though we'd be mutual poison
                  I can't rise
          to what impels you
              you've no fear
          of all the things my raising makes me shun
              how I'd resent that
                  how I do
                      poor boy
          though I see all that's fine it doesn't touch
          the nerve that tells me this is what I'm for
             that raw too stimulated spot that sparks
a longing I'd not harbour long except
      it's me
    it's in me like a germ
      and I'm
a puppet jumps when this live sore is touched
    how can I change and climb to where you are
we're sparrows

        we can't fly where eagles beat
we like our petty nests and fear the sheer
      cliff face where you must live alone because
            your nature's odd   we flock we're of a kind
    I'm like a million women and I'll chat
of carpets bathrooms mortgages and beds
just like a million men who blab of goals
        and is that you poor boy   will your mouth fill
    with emptiness like mine and not spit out
I know myself and what I'll grow into
    once I've kicked hopelessly against their pricks
      played out my wilful dumb-show in vain acts
            of false rejection of their settled ways
    I'll run in grooves that everybody knows
I need all others' notes to echo mine   or else I'm out of tune
    but you can sing
        a melody no-one has heard before
nor understands   and I can't harmonise.

  How do you float so lightly through your days
              how do you cheat
conceit and pride and show
    it undermines me how I can't learn how
  to live like that   as if tomorrow's all
you let today's advantage slip and pass
    won't stack your notes or climb into fixed place
      and in the fight between my sweet desire
and fear I couldn't keep you   wouldn't do
  what's sure wins out
    that's everything you hate
and call conceit and laugh at love to scoff
  why then I'll curl my lip and start to snarl
        why should I care for town and poor and fight
  to lift to where I am those who drag slow
    and heavy through a laboured life as if
      what they are touches me   our lives don't meet
we've made our way and leave them to make theirs
    all *we* have's well deserved   each brick each pound
to nature's best we've added effort's gild
    while they condemned by nature fail to thrive
  because their effort's paltry worthless shy
    I hate their town their terraced streets their yards
      their dirty backs
    their narrow trammelled lives
      I want this way of roses lilac lawn
  its mine by right   the sky itself says so

           each neutron and each proton spins for this
each step on history's path has led us here
        you're widdershins you'd try to cool the sun
it's nature's bidding makes their bid a farce
     and tragedy will fell you if you try to overturn its order
         streets are yours
    to walk with those you favour but not me
  I'll stay in avenues rich groves and drives.

     Poor boy say sweet girl to me one more time
then I'm away
          there's something of all time
       in you and my heart shrinks at what that might
           demand
       I'll take the route I know   it's safe
    away from town
       no crueller than I must
     to make myself a life here where I am
    I'll rise though some must fall to hold me up
      and what is that to me no more than you
   go to your town and try to lift your street
      I'll blend with those
     who'll use what means they must
   to keep streets in their place   and us in ours.

Town-boy the big square house has taught me this
    what's friendship set beside the gains of place
        that's what I am
     that's how my thoughts revolve
and when you're nowhere I'll look down on you
       and mock at friendship
    scoff at your loose ways
  a friend might let you down but money's sure
   what's love to this
  a quantity of worth no-one can hurt
    a wall a barrier
what can be added up is absolute
  I'll have my worth imposed hard-measured fixed
 should I depend on you what if you change
   I'll find that far-point where I can't be touched
  and stand behind my money like a god
        who am I   I'll say this much
        more than you
       I'd rather see the earth spin into dark
than give an inch of this my keep-out space
  who enters here is doomed for I admit

       no difference distance otherness or like
              I'm all and all my all is counted out in notes
      do some have more than I do then I'll fawn
        and crawling to ascend will say
           that all with less than me must do the same
          so you who laugh at coin and mock at place
       will find yourself excluded   spavined   trapped
you'll find what friendship means   when you're brought low
       for all eyes fix on rungs that rise above
           and all fear dogs-in-office more than death
      put friendship last ambition first's our creed
         you will go down poor boy   down to your street
        and we who rise with cynics' hard intent
will put our own advantage ever first   that's how our minds are made
           that's what we are
     we'll not be equals so we'll not be friends
our friendship's merely truce   uneasy   false
      all else would threaten all we've made of life
where each must battle each to prove their worth
     and proven worth puffs out its chest and gloats
but tells itself that all it own's deserved
  goodbye to friendship town-boy   kiss your street
 its concrete's not as hard as our fixed creed
   I'll find my way unfriended to high place.

  You'll fall   who'll catch you
     but the cruel street ?